NATIONAL
GEOGRAPHIC
KiDS

weird
but
true!

GROSS

NATIONAL
GEOGRAPHIC
KiDS

weird
but
true!

GROSS

NATIONAL GEOGRAPHIC
WASHINGTON, D.C.

HOUSEFLIES **VOMIT** DIGESTIVE **JUICES** ONTO THEIR FOOD, WHICH LIQUEFY THEIR MEALS SO THEY CAN SUCK THEM UP.

BY AGE **70,** THE AVERAGE PERSON HAS **SHED 105** POUNDS (48 KG) OF **SKIN.**

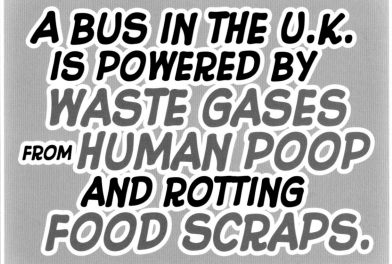

A BUS IN THE U.K. IS POWERED BY WASTE GASES FROM HUMAN POOP AND ROTTING FOOD SCRAPS.

GROSS

THAT'S GROSS!

RHINOS POOP IN PILES THAT ARE

TALLER THAN A TWO-YEAR-OLD.

THE GERMIEST PLACES IN A HOTEL ROOM? LIGHT SWITCHES AND TV REMOTES,

ACCORDING TO ONE STUDY.

THE U.S. FOOD AND DRUG ADMINISTRATION ALLOWS UP TO **19 MAGGOTS** AND **74 MITES** IN A SMALL CAN OF MUSHROOMS.

A COLLEGE FOOTBALL PLAYER **THREW UP** ON THE BALL DURING A CHAMPIONSHIP GAME—AND THEN SNAPPED IT TO THE QUARTERBACK.

IN CHINA, YOU CAN SIP **TEA MADE** FROM LEAVES **FERTILIZED** BY PANDA POOP.

NO, THANKS.

A FLOCK OF 50 CANADA GEESE CAN PRODUCE **5,000 POUNDS** (2,268 kg) **OF POOP** EACH YEAR

A group of **girls** in Nigeria developed a **pee-powered generator** that can provide **six hours of power on one quart (.95 L) of urine.**

THE MAIN INGREDIENT IN BIRD'S NEST SOUP, A COMMON DISH IN SOUTHEAST ASIA, IS **BIRD SPIT.**

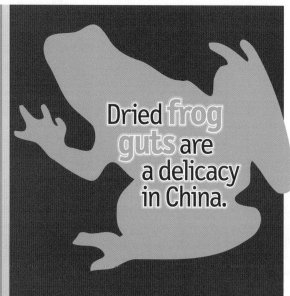

Dried **frog guts** are a delicacy in China.

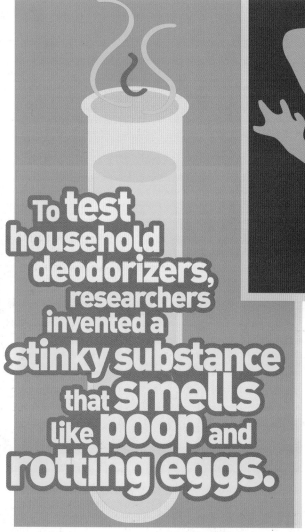

To **test household deodorizers,** researchers invented a **stinky substance** that **smells** like **poop** and **rotting eggs.**

Head lice can crawl at a speed of about nine inches [23 cm] per minute.

Your heart creates enough pressure to squirt blood up to 30 feet.

(9 m)

Your **nose** makes a fresh batch of **mucus** every **20 minutes.**

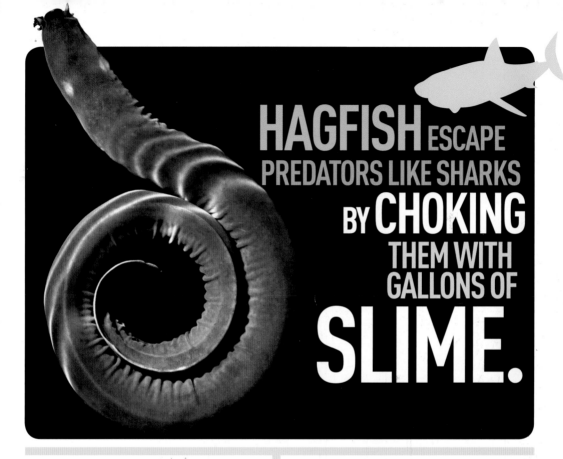

HAGFISH ESCAPE PREDATORS LIKE SHARKS BY **CHOKING** THEM WITH GALLONS OF **SLIME.**

Crocodiles can digest **bones** and horns.

Manatees use their toots to move up and down in the water.

BURROWING OWLS COLLECT
ANIMAL DROPPINGS
AND USE THEM AS BAIT TO ATTRACT ONE OF THEIR FAVORITE SNACKS:
POOP-SEEKING DUNG BEETLES.

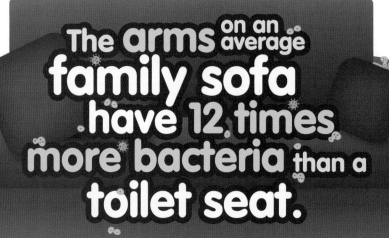

The **arms** on an average **family sofa** have 12 times more **bacteria** than a **toilet seat.**

THE **KISSING BUG** GETS ITS NAME BECAUSE IT OFTEN **BITES HUMANS AROUND THE MOUTH.**

THE CORPSE FLOWER, WHICH BLOOMS ONCE EVERY FEW YEARS, SMELLS LIKE ROTTING MEAT.

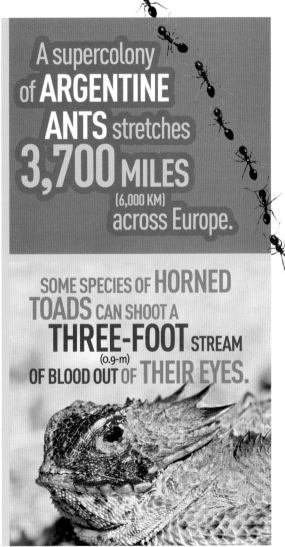

A supercolony of **ARGENTINE ANTS** stretches **3,700** MILES (6,000 KM) across Europe.

SOME SPECIES OF **HORNED TOADS** CAN SHOOT A **THREE-FOOT** STREAM (0.9-m) OF BLOOD OUT OF **THEIR EYES.**

21

Among the artifacts at the Mütter Museum, in Philadelphia, Pennsylvania, U.S.A., you will find jars of picked human skin and bedbugs extracted from a person's ear.

MOST PEOPLE TOOT 6 TO 20 TIMES A DAY.

MARINE IGUANAS
SNEEZE SALT
ONTO THEIR HEADS TO FORM SMALL WHITE
"WIGS."

25

THE AVERAGE BELLY BUTTON IS HOME TO 67 DIFFERENT SPECIES OF BACTERIA.

AN **ENTOMOLOGIST** **LET** **BOTFLY LARVAE** LIVE UNDER HIS SKIN FOR TWO MONTHS AND THEN MADE A VIDEO OF THE **MAGGOT CRAWLING** UT.

THE SURFACE AREA OF YOUR SMALL INTESTINE IS ABOUT THE SIZE OF A TENNIS COURT.

THE BOMBARDIER BEETLE **SQUIRTS A TOXIC,** BOILING-HOT FLUID FROM ITS REAR END.

A DUNG BEETLE CAN MOVE A BALL OF POOP 50 TIMES ITS OWN BODY WEIGHT.

The **tufted titmouse** lines its nest with hair plucked from the tails of ROADKILL SQUIRRELS.

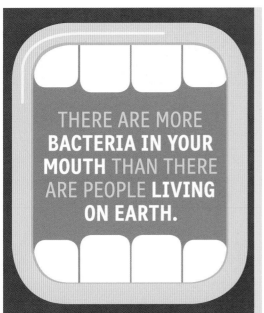

THERE ARE MORE **BACTERIA IN YOUR MOUTH** THAN THERE ARE PEOPLE **LIVING ON EARTH.**

TERMITES USE THEIR **OWN POOP** AS BUILDING MATERIAL FOR THEIR NESTS.

An Italian man once produced a burp lasting **1 minute 13.057 seconds** —the longest belch on record.

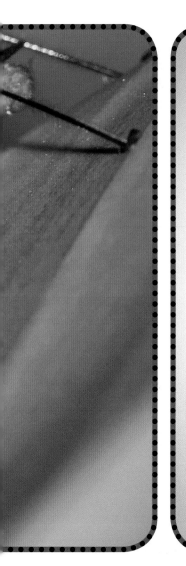

THE ASSASSIN BUG STABS ITS PREY, SUCKS OUT WHAT IT WANTS TO EAT, AND WEARS THE CORPSE ON ITS BACK.

SWEAT HAS NO SCENT. **BACTERIA ON YOUR** SKIN MIX WITH SWEAT AND MAKE IT **STINKY.**

SOME MITES FEAST ON THE OOZE IN RABBITS' EARS.

To deter predators, opossums sometimes DROOL and LIE STIFFLY, trying to look too SICK TO EAT.

COUGH

35

The **World's largest** **earthworm** is about **three feet** (0.9 m) long and sounds like a draining bathtub when moving through soil.

THAT'S GROSS!

ROACHES SOMETIMES EAT HAIR, SEWAGE, AND GLUE.

Your brain is the texture of tofu.

Lions cough up hair balls the size of hot dogs.

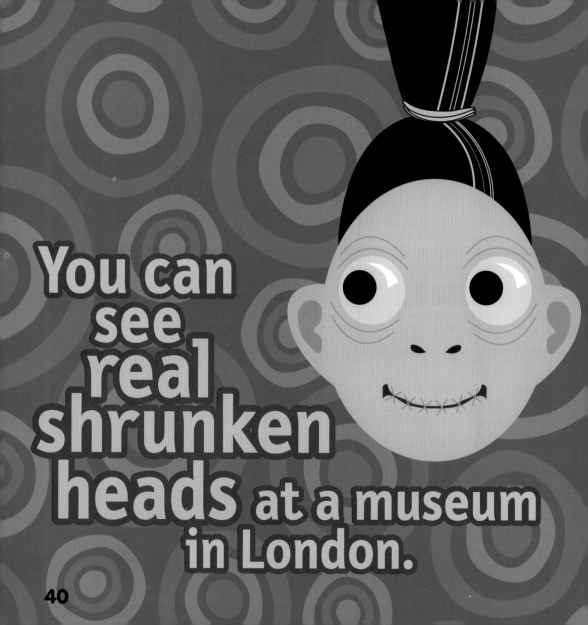

You can see real shrunken heads at a museum in London.

LARVAE OF THE **NEW WORLD SCREWWORM** HAVE A SPIRAL SHAPE THAT ALLOWS THEM TO TUNNEL INTO FLESH.

RATS CAN'T

SEWER INSPECTORS
WADE THROUGH RAW SEWAGE AND
dodge rats!
TO FIX CRACKED AND CLOGGED PIPES.

VOMIT.

THERE
ARE ABOUT
two million
RATS IN NEW YORK CITY.

The Morbid Anatomy Museum in Brooklyn, New York, U.S.A., once displayed a brooch made of **human teeth.**

THE WORLD'S LARGEST COLLECTION OF **TOENAIL CLIPPINGS CONTAINS** SAMPLES FROM **24,999** PEOPLE.

SOME PEOPLE CAN BELCH OUT BURPS REGISTERING MORE THAN 100 DECIBELS—THAT'S LOUDER THAN A ROARING MOTORCYCLE!

A VENUS FLYTRAP CAN DIGEST A FROG.

AN ASSASSIN SPIDER IMPALES ITS VICTIM, INJECTS IT WITH VENOM, AND LETS IT DANGLE UNTIL IT DIES.

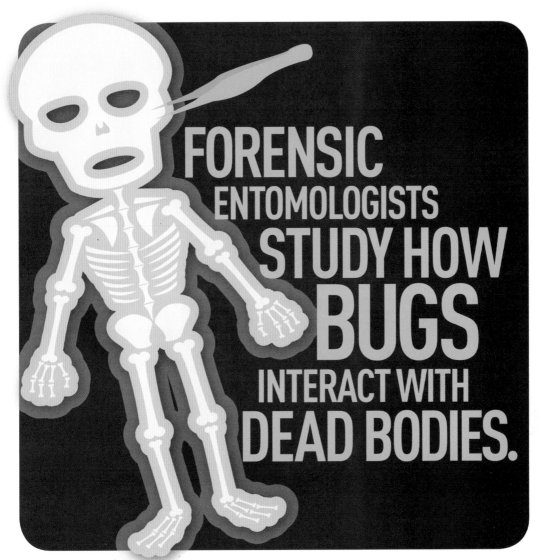

FORENSIC ENTOMOLOGISTS STUDY HOW BUGS INTERACT WITH DEAD BODIES.

ACCORDING TO
ONE IN FIVE ADULTS HAS PEED WHILE

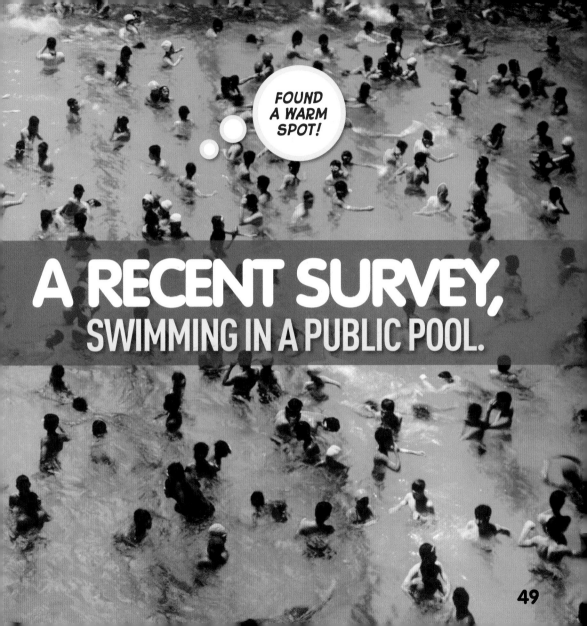

Some **tiny snails** can **survive** being **eaten by birds** —and are found alive in their **poop!**

A restaurant owner in England created the **"PIE-SCRAPER,"** a burger that is **5 feet 4 inches** (1.6 m) **tall,** made from more than **18 pounds** (8.5 kg) of meat, and contains **30,000 calories.**

Bacteria can linger on airplane tray tables for three days.

Some red-tinted foods—like candies, yogurt, and ketchup—get their bright hue from the crushed belly of a bug.

In Vietnam, a serving of a **snake's** still-beating heart is considered a delicacy.

In Alaska, U.S.A., you can snack on "ESKIMO ICE CREAM" —a frozen mix of REINDEER FAT, SEAL OIL, GROUND FISH, FRESH BERRIES, and SNOW.

EXCRETIONS FROM A BEAVER'S BEHIND HAVE BEEN USED TO GIVE FOOD

A STRAWBERRY OR RASPBERRY FLAVOR.

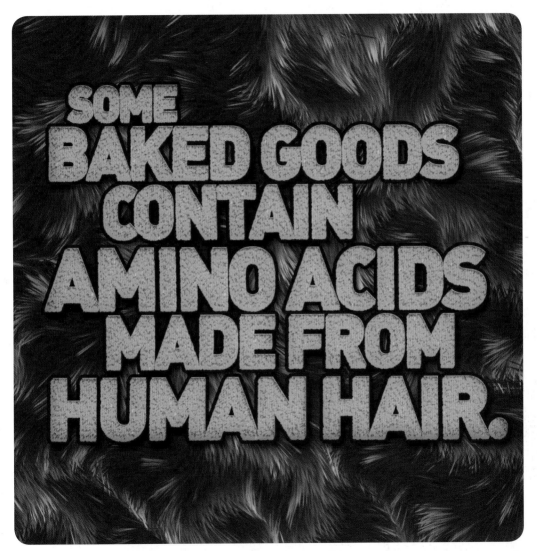

SOME BAKED GOODS CONTAIN AMINO ACIDS MADE FROM HUMAN HAIR.

Much of **Hawaii's beaches** are made from the **poop** of parrotfish, sea urchins, and worms.

AT ONE TIME, EUROPEAN ROYALTY TOOK MEDICINE MADE FROM HUMAN BONES, BLOOD, AND FAT TO TREAT HEADACHES AND OTHER AILMENTS.

You can eat a **dessert** called **"bloody poop"** out of a **toilet-shaped bowl** at the **Modern Toilet Restaurant** in Kaohsiung, Taiwan.

JELL-O ONCE CAME IN **COFFEE, CELERY,** AND **SEASONED TOMATO FLAVORS.**

Mites live in the hair follicles of your eyelashes.

HÁKARL, A NATIONAL DISH OF ICELAND, IS MADE FROM ROTTEN, FERMENTED SHARK MEAT.

PALEOSCATOLOGISTS=
SCIENTISTS WHO STUDY FOSSILIZED
DUNG

One man's **ear hairs** measured **7.1** inches (18 cm) long.

 You can find a 40-year-old **Twinkie** at a high school in Maine, U.S.A.—  it's housed in a glass box and is surprisingly mold free!

IN HOT CONDITIONS, A LINEMAN IN FOOTBALL MAY LOSE UP TO **NINE POUNDS** (4 kg) OF SWEAT IN ONE GAME.

A French company sells canned **edible insects,** including **cheese-and-bacon-flavored waterbugs,** barbecue black scorpions, and **wasabi mealworms.**

AT BUG-THEMED **"PESTAURANTS,"** YOU CAN DINE ON GRASSHOPPER BURGERS, ROASTED CRICKETS, AND **ANT** LOLLIPOPS.

A man from India once sucked **509** fish through his mouth and snorted them out his nose in one hour.

BASEBALL PLAYER **LUIS GONZALEZ'S** CHEWED BUBBLE GUM ONCE SOLD AT AN AUCTION FOR **$10,000.**

THE SPITBALL, BANNED ALMOST A CENTURY AGO, WAS A BASEBALL COVERED IN SALIVA THAT MADE THE **BALL HARDER TO HIT.**

SCUBA DIVERS IN THE CARIBBEAN GOT CAUGHT IN A 100-FOOT (30-M)-WIDE **"POONADO"** OF WHALE WASTE.

BEDBUGS, HEAD LICE, AND FLEAS HAVE BEEN FOUND PRESERVED IN ANCIENT **EGYPTIAN TOMBS.**

A Missouri, U.S.A., barber created a HAIR BALL WEIGHING **167 POUNDS** (75.7 kg) AND STANDING **FOUR FEET** TALL (1.2 m)

At the World Pigs' Feet Eating Championship in New Jersey, U.S.A., participants competed by eating boiled pigs' parts sprayed with lemon juice.

A GERMAN MAN SUCKED DOWN **14 OUNCES** (396 G) OF **KETCHUP** THROUGH A **STRAW** IN JUST 32.37 **SECONDS.**

A typical mattress contains between 100,000 and 10 million dust mites.

IN WISCONSIN, U.S.A., YOU CAN ENTER A "COW CHIP" THROWING COMPETITION WHERE CONTESTANTS FLING DRIED COW POOP.

A British man ate 36 live cockroaches in one minute.

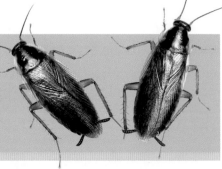

A 19TH-CENTURY ENGLISHMAN NAMED JAMES LUCAS DIDN'T BATHE FOR 25 YEARS.

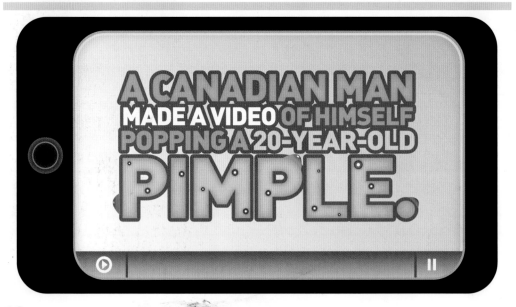

A CANADIAN MAN MADE A VIDEO OF HIMSELF POPPING A 20-YEAR-OLD PIMPLE.

WORMZELS = WORMS TWISTED INTO A PRETZEL SHAPE AND BAKED.

VAMPIRE FINCHES DRINK THE BLOOD OF OTHER BIRDS.

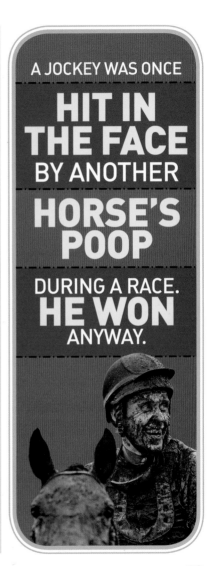

A JOCKEY WAS ONCE **HIT IN THE FACE** BY ANOTHER **HORSE'S POOP** DURING A RACE. **HE WON** ANYWAY.

A man in China can **pull a car** by hooking ropes onto **his lower eyelids.**

A woman in Las Vegas, Nevada, U.S.A., has fingernails that are **longer than** your entire **arm.**

71

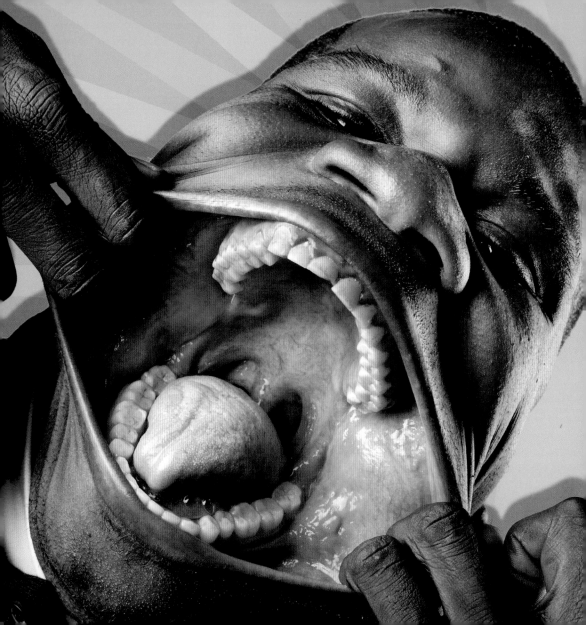

A man nicknamed the "Angolan Jaw of Awe" can open his mouth 6.7 inches— (17 cm) wide enough to cram an entire soda can in sideways.

During the **1500s,** Brits soaked their *fabrics* in *stale urine* to help bind **color dyes** to cloth.

THE BAGS IN **ESTONIAN BAGPIPES**, CALLED TORUPILLS, WERE ORIGINALLY MADE FROM SEALS' STOMACHS.

AN **ADULT'S** BLADDER CAN HOLD TWO CUPS OF **URINE**. (473 ML)

In the 1700s, some people believed that the **touch of a dead man's hand** could cure cysts and warts.

75

Some ancient Romans used *powdered mouse brains* as toothpaste.

Women in ancient Rome dyed their hair with *goat fat and ashes* from burned wood.

Ancient Romans used urine to whiten their teeth.

In ancient Rome, people socialized at open-air public toilets, some of which could "seat" up to 80 people at a time.

Instead of using toilet paper, ancient Romans would wipe with a shared sponge on a stick.

A man in **China** **once** **stuck** a total of **2,188** needles into his **head** **and** **face.**

A WOMAN IN CHICAGO, ILLINOIS, U.S.A., CAN POP HER EYEBALLS **0.47 INCHES** (12 mm) OUT OF HER EYE SOCKETS.

An Australian man **COLLECTED** his belly button lint for **26 YEARS**— and plucked **ENOUGH FLUFF TO FILL THREE JARS.**

For her job as a **FOOT-CARE PRODUCT TESTER**, an Ohio, U.S.A., woman sniffed **5,600 FEET.**

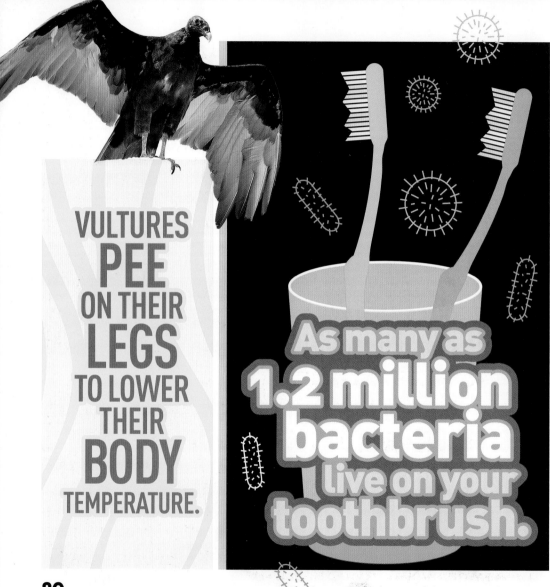

VULTURES **PEE** ON THEIR **LEGS** TO LOWER THEIR **BODY** TEMPERATURE.

As many as **1.2 million bacteria** live on your **toothbrush.**

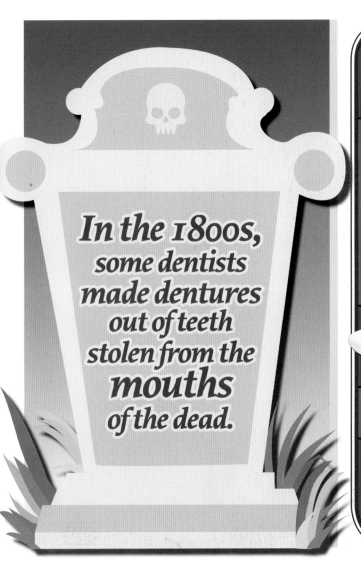

In the 1800s, some dentists made dentures out of teeth stolen from the **mouths** of the dead.

A SHEEP'S **STOMACH** STUFFED WITH THE SHEEP'S LIVER, LUNGS, AND HEART, PLUS ONIONS, SPICES, AND OATMEAL

=

HAGGIS, A NATIONAL DISH OF SCOTLAND

81

A camel's "spit" is partly digested food it burps up and hurls when it feels threatened.

A **MOUSE** CAN SQUEEZE THROUGH

A **H**  **LE**

THE SIZE OF A NICKEL.
FOR RATS, THE HOLE NEEDS TO BE THE SIZE OF HALF A QUARTER.

A CLUMP OF CONGEALED COOKING OIL THE **SIZE OF A JUMBO JET** WAS ONCE REMOVED FROM LONDON'S SEWER SYSTEM.

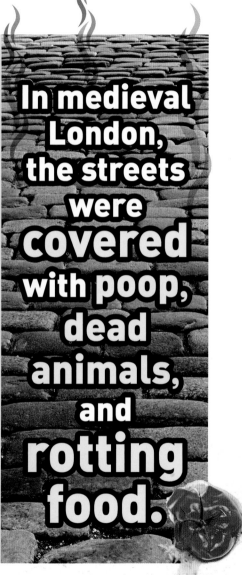

In medieval London, the streets were **covered** with poop, dead animals, and **rotting food.**

THE **DECEASED BODY** OF 11TH-CENTURY ENGLISH KING WILLIAM THE CONQUEROR REPORTEDLY **EXPLODED** AS IT WAS BEING STUFFED INTO A **COFFIN.**

A BABY'S FIRST POOP IS BLACK AND STICKY LIKE TAR.

Many ribbon **worms can regrow** chopped-off body parts **into new worms—** one six-inch (15-cm) worm can turn into **more than 200,000!**

Crocodiles sometimes foam around the eyes when they eat.

A FUNGUS IN THE BRAZILIAN RAIN FOREST INVADES **ANTS' BRAINS** AND **TURNS** THEM INTO **ZOMBIES.**

TERMITES CAN TOOT SO FORCEFULLY THAT THEIR ABDOMENS EXPLODE.

ANCIENT EGYPTIANS TOOK BATHS IN BLOOD, BELIEVING IT WAS GOOD FOR THEIR HEALTH.

Ancient Egyptians tossed their waste into the Nile River—and then used the same water for drinking and bathing.

KING TUT WAS BURIED WITH 145 PAIRS OF UNDERWEAR.

To fight baldness, ancient Egyptians covered their heads with a mixture of the fat of hippos, crocodiles, snakes, tomcats, and ibexes.

TO MAKE A MUMMY, ANCIENT EGYPTIANS WOULD FIRST PULL THE BRAIN OF THE DECEASED OUT THROUGH THE NOSE.

TICKBIRDS
EAT FLIES, MAGGOTS, AND TICKS OFF THE HIDES OF RHINOS.

WHEN YOU GET A SCRAPE IN SPACE, BLOOD DOESN'T RUN DOWN YOUR SKIN—IT FORMS INTO A BLOB OVER THE CUT.

Vampire bats' only food is blood.

An engineer invented a machine that turns POOP INTO clean drinking WATER.

A British man had a parasitic worm living in his brain for four years.

CHAMPION SPEED EATER MATT STONIE CAN DOWN 62 HOT DOGS— AND BUNS—IN TEN MINUTES!

Thief ants eat kitchen grease and dead rodents.

THAT'S WEIRD!

75 PERCENT of Americans admit to using their phones in the bathroom.

DURIAN, A TROPICAL FRUIT FOUND IN SOUTHEAST ASIA, **HAS THE TEXTURE OF** CUSTARD AND **SMELLS LIKE ROTTING GARBAGE.**

A man in Maryland, U.S.A., once plowed snow using a motorized toilet.

AMERICAN CROCODILES THROW UP BITS OF FOOD TO ATTRACT FISH THEY WANT TO EAT.

Medieval women used **SULFUR** to try to burn off their **FRECKLES.**

April 23 is International Nose Picking Day.

Black pudding, a breakfast staple in England and Ireland, is **sausage made from** onions, fat, and **pigs' blood.**

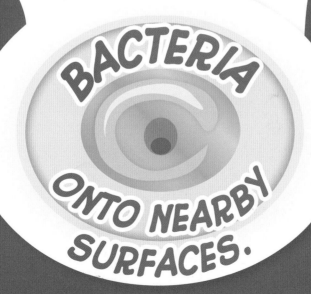

FLUSHING THE TOILET WITH THE LID UP CAN PROPEL BACTERIA ONTO NEARBY SURFACES.

A COMPANY IN BROOKLYN, NEW YORK, U.S.A., SPECIALIZES IN **SCRAPING GUM** OFF CITY SIDEWALKS.

SCIENTISTS FOUND A **1,000-YEAR-OLD MUMMIFIED MONK** INSIDE A STATUE OF A SITTING BUDDHA.

Hippos make their own **sunscreen** by oozing a thick red substance called **"blood sweat."**

Sharks **pee through** their skin.

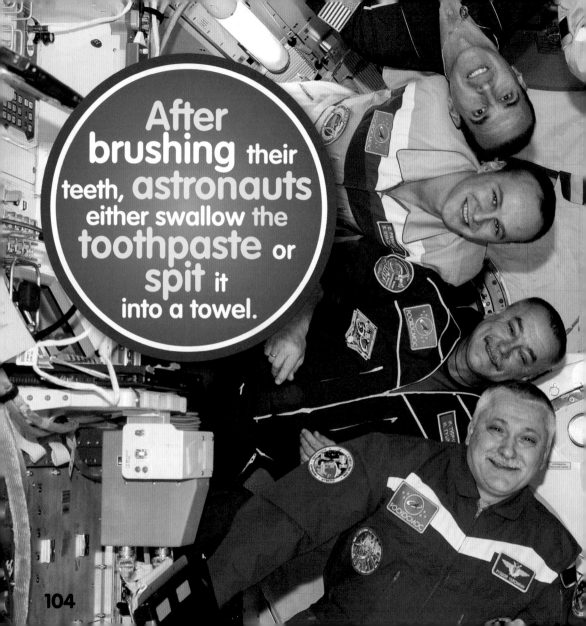

After **brushing** their teeth, **astronauts** either swallow the **toothpaste** or **spit** it into a towel.

Astronauts train in an airsickness-inducing flight simulator nicknamed the "vomit comet."

TO MAKE THEIR PUPILS LARGER—A MARK OF BEAUTY AT THE TIME— SOME MEDIEVAL ITALIAN WOMEN DROPPED THE JUICE OF THE POISONOUS NIGHTSHADE PLANT INTO THEIR EYES.

A MUSEUM ABOUT THE PARIS SEWER SYSTEM IS LOCATED INSIDE THE PARIS SEWER.

At a London café, diners eat in booths that used to be urinals.

To stay warm in winter, children in England during the Middle Ages were often **sewn into their clothes**— not changing them for months at a time.

Some ancient soldiers drank the

BLOOD

of the first opponent they killed on the battlefield.

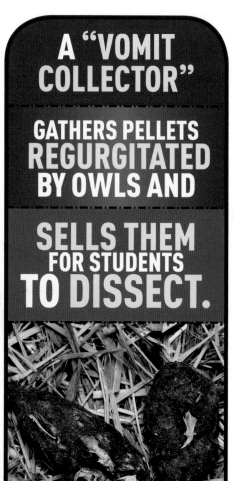

A "VOMIT COLLECTOR"

GATHERS PELLETS **REGURGITATED BY OWLS AND**

SELLS THEM FOR STUDENTS **TO DISSECT.**

An Austrian woman invented a **maggot-breeding home appliance** so people could dine on protein-rich larvae.

SCIENTISTS CAN STUDY POLLUTION BY EXAMINING THE EARWAX OF BLUE WHALES.

The average home creates **40 pounds** (18 kg) of dust every year.

Dust mites eat the dead

One speck of dust contains **40,000** dust mites.

skin of pets and people.

Monkeys pick **dead skin, dirt, and bugs** out of one another's fur.

WHEN DWARF BOAS ARE THREATENED, THEIR EYES FILL WITH BLOOD.

Before toilets were developed, people emptied chamber pots filled with urine out their windows onto city streets.

Ten-inch-long Giant African land snails (25-cm) were found **eating stucco off the sides of houses** in Miami, Florida, U.S.A.

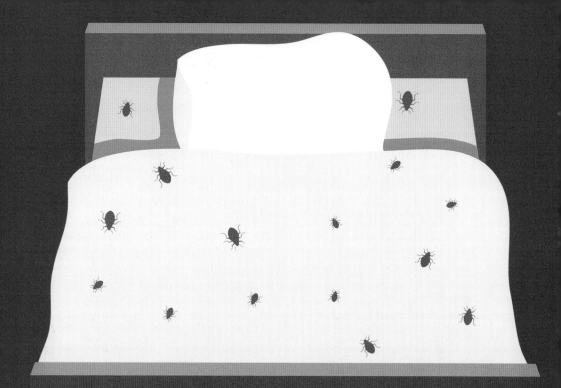

BEDBUGS POOP
BLOOD SPOTS NEAR WHERE THEY HIDE OUT AND FEED.

HIGH LEVELS OF METHANE GAS RELEASED FROM THE BURPS AND TOOTS OF 90 COWS CAUSED A BARN IN GERMANY TO EXPLODE.

When attacked, sea cucumbers turn their bodies inside out and eject their guts.

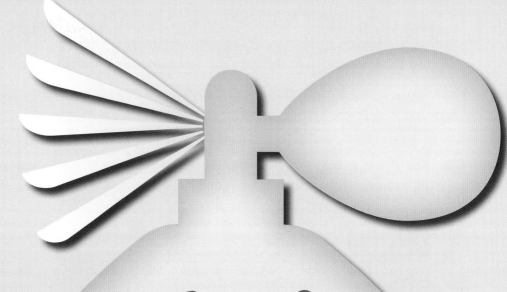

Ambergris= the intestinal gunk of **sperm whales** that is used in some **perfumes**

AN AVERAGE ADULT **PEES ENOUGH EVERY YEAR** TO FILL A **150-GALLON** (568-L) **HOME AQUARIUM.**

SPANISH RIBBED NEWTS **CAN THRUST THEIR RIBS** THROUGH THEIR **SKIN AND** USE THEM AS **WEAPONS.**

Giraffes sometimes use their long tongues to clean their ears and noses.

SLUGS **BREATHE THROUGH** A HOLE **IN THE SIDE** OF THEIR **BODIES.**

ONE OUT OF **TEN BRITISH TRAINS** EMPTIES **TOILET WASTE** RIGHT ONTO THE **RAILWAY TRACKS.**

A MUSEUM IN TURKEY DISPLAYS AN ESTIMATED **16,000 LOCKS** OF **HAIR** LEFT BY ITS VISITORS.

DROPLETS FROM YOUR **SNEEZES** CAN HANG IN THE AIR FOR **20 MINUTES.**

AUSTRALIAN WOMBATS PRODUCE CUBE-SHAPED POOP.

Teenagers **pick their noses** an **average** of **four times** a day.

43 percent of kids pick off their scabs.

10 PERCENT OF KIDS SAY THEY CHEW ON THEIR TOENAILS!

A TYPE OF **LOUSE** INFESTS A **FISH'S MOUTH, EATS ITS TONGUE,** AND **LIVES THERE** AS THE FISH'S NEW TONGUE.

To help swallow its meal, one species of frog pulls its eyes into the roof of its mouth.

YOUR BODY PRODUCES UP TO 8 CUPS (2 L) OF SPIT A DAY.

Leopard geckos **pee** solid **crystals** instead of **liquid urine.**

PENGUIN PARENTS REGURGITATE FOOD INTO THEIR BABIES' MOUTHS.

Sloths poop only once a week.

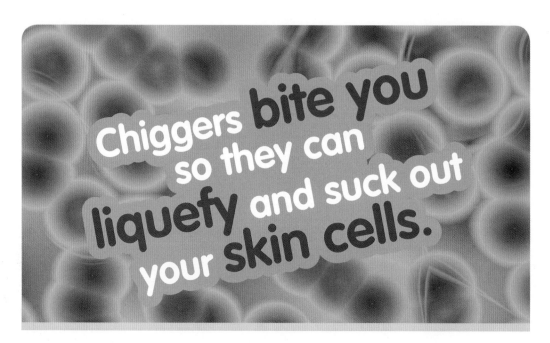

Chiggers bite you so they can liquefy and suck out your skin cells.

The air you spew during a  travels **faster than a car racing down a highway.**

Vampire spiders eat blood-engorged mosquito abdomens.

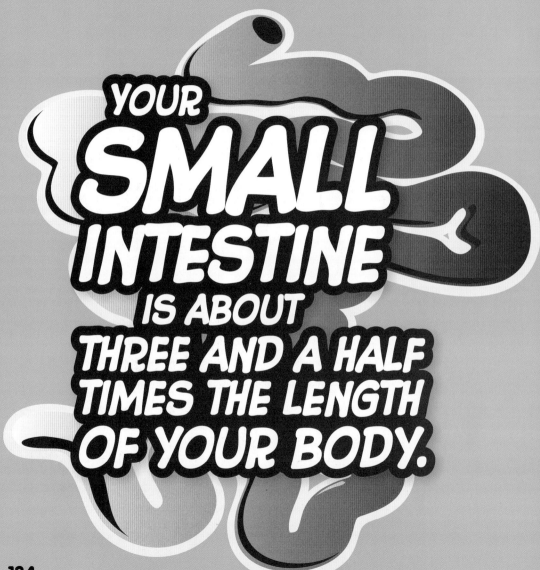

YOUR **SMALL INTESTINE** IS ABOUT THREE AND A HALF TIMES THE LENGTH OF YOUR BODY.

SOME SUGAR IS FILTERED AND BLEACHED WITH CHARRED ANIMAL BONES!

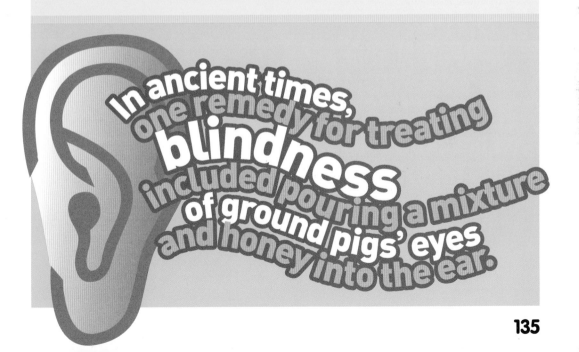

In ancient times, one remedy for treating **blindness** included pouring a mixture of ground pigs' eyes and honey into the ear.

135

In England, a vial of blood from former British prime minister **Winston Churchill** was put up for auction.

To get rid of a **GUINEA WORM—** A PARASITE that can grow as LONG AS **THREE FEET** (0.9 m)— you have to wait until IT CRAWLS OUT OF A BLISTER formed ON YOUR SKIN.

Skipper caterpillars can **shoot out poop** pellets as far as **40** times their body length.

TOE JAM =
THE SOCK LINT, DIRT, BACTERIA, SKIN CELLS, AND **FUNGUS** THAT BUILDS UP BETWEEN YOUR TOES

IN JAPAN, YOU CAN GET A SPA TREATMENT IN WHICH SNAILS CRAWL ACROSS YOUR FACE AND LEAVE TRAILS OF SLIME.

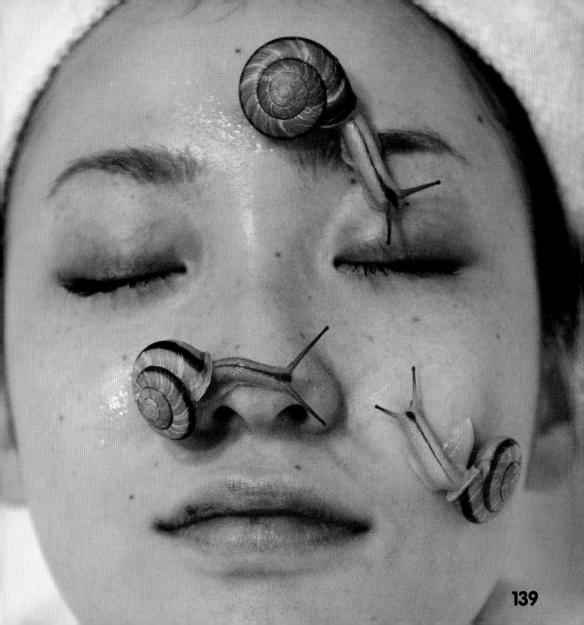

AFTER A FROG SHEDS ITS SKIN, IT EATS IT!

IN THE 1800S, SOME PEOPLE USED EARWAX AS LIP BALM.

One species of turtle pees from its mouth.

THAT'S GROSS!

THE ACID IN YOUR STOMACH CAN DISSOLVE METAL.

HOOK-WORMS

CAN ENTER **YOUR BODY**

THROUGH YOUR FEET AND GROW IN YOUR INTESTINES.

TURKEY VULTURES CAN **DETECT THE ODOR** OF **ROTTING FLESH** FROM MORE THAN **A MILE AWAY.**
(1.6 km)

Cockroaches can **live** for weeks **without** a **HEAD.**

143

A TYPE OF BEE FEEDS ON HUMAN TEARS.

A **man** successfully **treated** his intestinal disease by **ingesting 1,500** parasitic **worm eggs.**

HAIR GROWS EVERYWHERE ON YOUR BODY

EXCEPT FOR YOUR PALMS, LIPS, EYELIDS, AND THE SOLES OF YOUR FEET.

95 PERCENT OF PEOPLE DON'T WASH THEIR HANDS LONG ENOUGH TO KILL INFECTIOUS GERMS AFTER USING THE TOILET— AND 10 PERCENT DON'T WASH THEIR HANDS AT ALL!

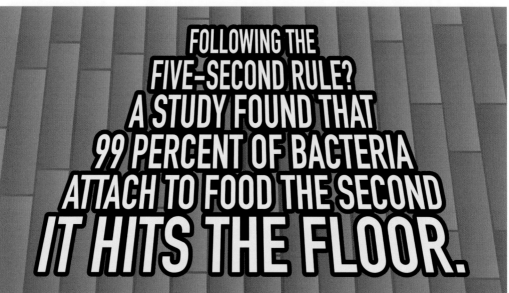

FOLLOWING THE FIVE-SECOND RULE? A STUDY FOUND THAT 99 PERCENT OF BACTERIA ATTACH TO FOOD THE SECOND *IT HITS THE FLOOR.*

Bites from fire ants **cause pus-filled blisters** that **can last** for **a week.**

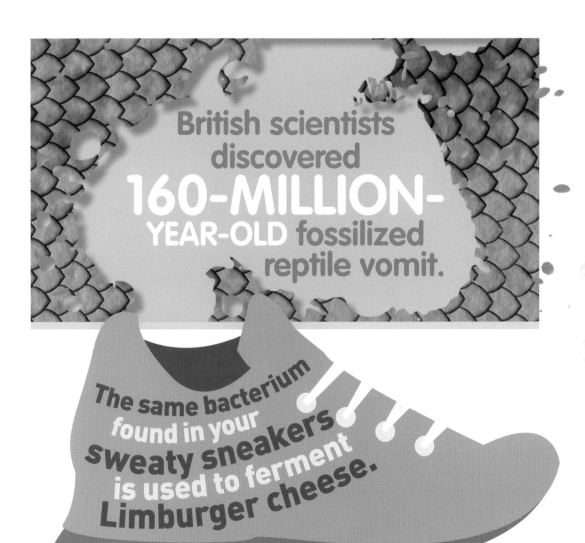

British scientists discovered **160-MILLION-YEAR-OLD** fossilized reptile vomit.

The same bacterium found in your sweaty sneakers is used to ferment Limburger cheese.

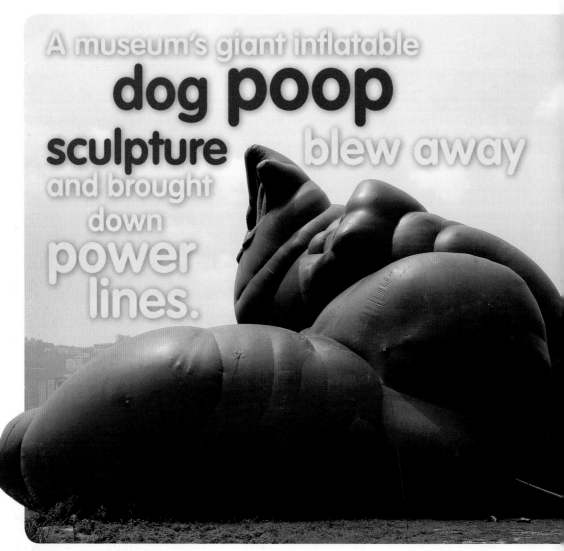

A museum's giant inflatable **dog poop** **sculpture** **blew away** and brought down **power** **lines.**

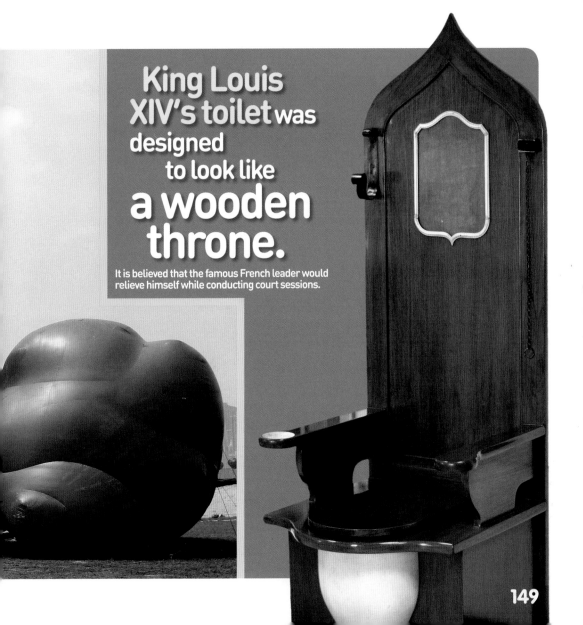

King Louis XIV's toilet was designed to look like a wooden throne.

It is believed that the famous French leader would relieve himself while conducting court sessions.

149

Sea pig =

a type of sea cucumber that feasts on whale carcasses that have fallen to the ocean floor

YUM!

SOME WOMEN IN ANCIENT EGYPT USED EYE MAKEUP MADE FROM CRUSHED ANT EGGS.

A WOMAN IN 17TH-CENTURY FRANCE REPORTEDLY SHED HORNS— INCLUDING ONE 12 INCHES (30 cm) LONG!—FROM HER FOREHEAD.

BATHING WAS ONCE CONSIDERED BAD FOR YOUR HEALTH.

BOOGERS ARE THE **DUST, POLLEN, SAND, DIRT, AND OTHER MATERIALS** THAT GET TRAPPED BY YOUR MUCUS.

DURING BATTLES, MEDIEVAL KNIGHTS HAD TO RELIEVE THEIR BLADDERS AND BOWELS INSIDE THEIR ARMOR.

A COMPANY IN
WALES
MAKES PAPER
OUT OF SHEEP
POO.

PEACOCKS

THAT'S GROSS!

COOKED IN THEIR **FEATHERS** WERE SERVED AT MEDIEVAL BANQUETS.

ABOUT ONE IN FIVE PEOPLE HAVE DROPPED THEIR PHONE INTO A TOILET.

DON'T LOOK AT ME!

A CHEMICAL FOUND IN ANTIFREEZE IS USED TO THICKEN SOME SALAD DRESSINGS.

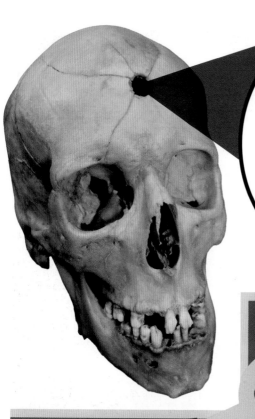

DOCTORS IN ANCIENT PERU **DRILLED HOLES** IN PATIENTS' SKULLS TO RELIEVE THEIR HEADACHES.

SNAIL SLIME WAS USED AS **COUGH SYRUP** IN THE MIDDLE AGES.

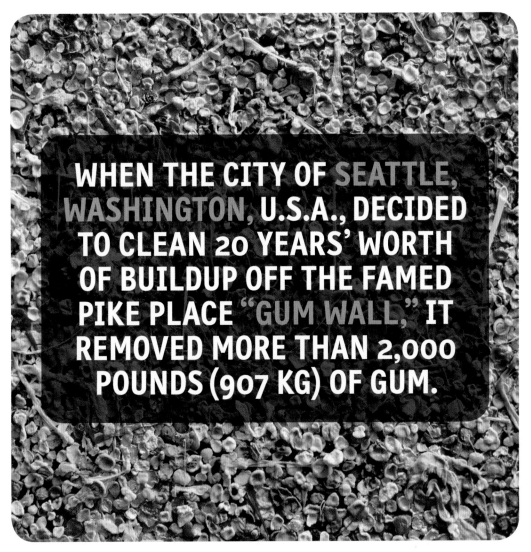

WHEN THE CITY OF SEATTLE, WASHINGTON, U.S.A., DECIDED TO CLEAN 20 YEARS' WORTH OF BUILDUP OFF THE FAMED PIKE PLACE "GUM WALL," IT REMOVED MORE THAN 2,000 POUNDS (907 KG) OF GUM.

A British man found a dead mouse baked into a loaf of bread he was using to make sandwiches.

PEOPLE ONCE **SPREAD COW POOP** ON THEIR **FLOORS TO DISCOURAGE** DISEASE-CARRYING FLEAS.

THAT'S WEIRD!

IT DIDN'T WORK.

Picking your nose

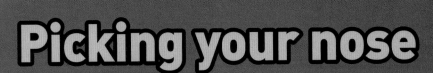

in public was acceptable

during the Middle Ages.

FRIED GRASSHOPPERS ARE SAID TO TASTE LIKE SPICY POPCORN.

ANCIENT GREEK DOCTOR HIPPOCRATES DIAGNOSED HIS PATIENTS BY TASTING THEIR EARWAX AND SMELLING THEIR POOP.

SOME EXPERTS CLAIM THAT THE GIANT WATER BUG TASTES LIKE A JOLLY RANCHER.

161

AN EYEBALL THE SIZE OF A **SOFTBALL** ONCE WASHED UP ON THE **BEACH** IN FORT LAUDERDALE, FLORIDA, U.S.A.

In the Welsh sport of **bog snorkeling, contestants compete to swim the fastest** through **cold, murky, foul-smelling water.**

U.S. GOVERNMENT **REGULATIONS ALLOW UP TO** ONE RODENT HAIR IN EVERY 3.5 OUNCES (100 g) OF PEANUT BUTTER SOLD.

THERE MAY BE UP TO **30 FLY EGGS** IN EVERY 3.5 OUNCES (100 G) OF **PIZZA SAUCE.**

LARGE GOBS OF TANGLED WORMS

ONCE FELL FROM THE SKY IN JENNINGS, LOUISIANA, U.S.A.

FISH SCALES ARE SOMETIMES USED TO MAKE SHIMMERY LIPSTICK AND NAIL POLISH.

A WOMAN WON AN ANNUAL

"BOOGER SHOOTING CONTEST"

BY SENDING HER SNOT ALMOST 20 FEET (6 M) ACROSS A ROOM.

Doctors removed a nine-pound (4.1-kg) **hair ball** from a teenage girl's **stomach.**

A man's **ear canal** became infested with hundreds of **maggots** after a housefly laid eggs in it while he slept.

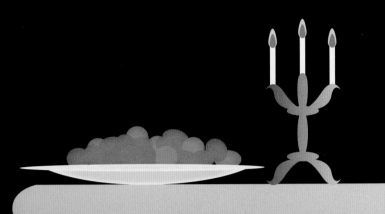

Sweetbreads=
*fried glands
or organs of*
**cows, pigs,
or lambs**

AN ELEPHANT'S EYE CAN BE AS BIG AS YOUR FIST.

For more than **30 years,** a British man has eaten a diet of **roadkill meat,** whipping up dishes like **fox lasagna and frog leg stir-fry.**

A woman spent 33 days in a room filled with more than

5,000 SCORPIONS.

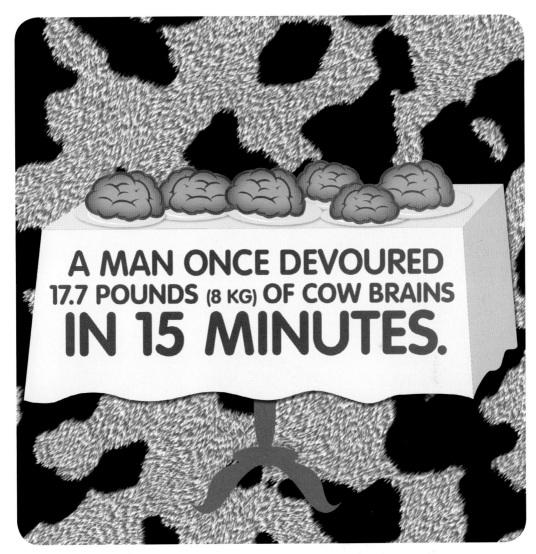

A MAN ONCE DEVOURED 17.7 POUNDS (8 KG) OF COW BRAINS IN 15 MINUTES.

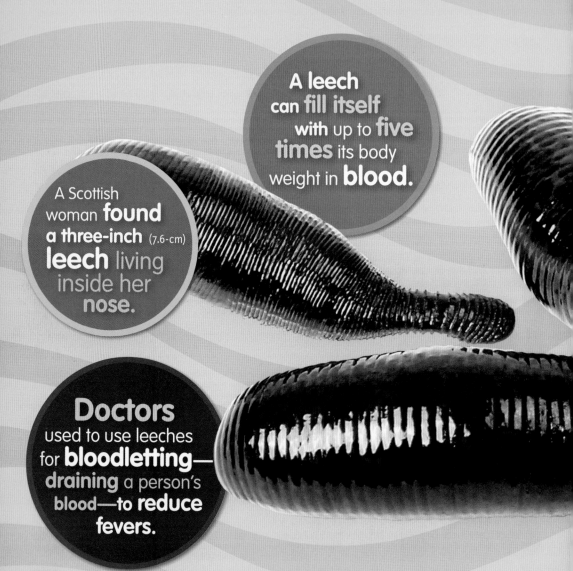

A leech can **fill itself** with up to **five times** its body weight in **blood.**

A Scottish woman **found a three-inch** (7.6-cm) **leech** living inside her **nose.**

Doctors used to use leeches for **bloodletting**—**draining** a person's blood—**to reduce fevers.**

In the **Middle Ages,** "leech collectors" would wade **in ponds, let leeches** attach to their bare legs, and then **sell them** for **medical** use.

The world's **largest leech** can **grow** to be **as long as** two pencils!

173

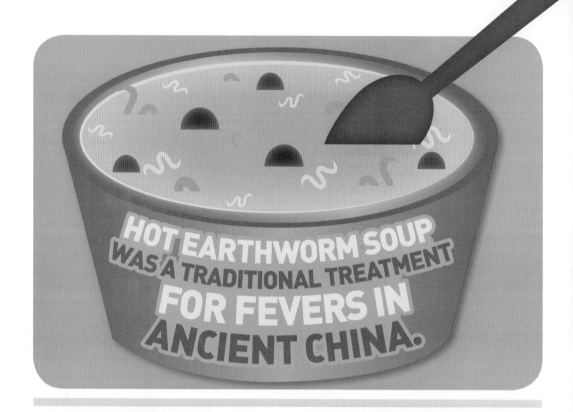

HOT EARTHWORM SOUP WAS A TRADITIONAL TREATMENT FOR FEVERS IN ANCIENT CHINA.

SOME HOSPITALS USE **FLESH-EATING MAGGOTS** TO TREAT INFECTED WOUNDS.

THE ANNUAL BUG BOWL COMPETITION IN INDIANA, U.S.A., FEATURES A CRICKET-SPITTING CONTEST.

You can see real **human and animal bodies** preserved in

PLASTIC

at the **Plastinarium** in Guben, Germany.

If it weren't for a layer of **sticky mucus** on its walls, **your stomach** would **digest itself.**

THE ENTIRE TOWN OF **ROTORUA, NEW ZEALAND** —KNOWN AS THE **"STINK CAPITAL OF THE WORLD"** —SMELLS LIKE **ROTTEN EGGS.**

A PERFORMANCE ARTIST HAD A THIRD EAR IMPLANTED ON HIS FOREARM.

AN AUSTRALIAN ARTIST MAKES **JEWELRY** OUT OF *HUMAN HAIR,* *TEETH,* AND **NAIL CLIPPINGS.**

Most of the dust flecks you see in a sunbeam are shed dead skin.

A CALIFORNIA, U.S.A., MAN MADE A BOLOGNA, CHEESE, AND LETTUCE SANDWICH IN 1 MINUTE 57 SECONDS USING ONLY HIS HIS FEET.

The *Rotten* Sneaker Contest offers cash prizes to kids with the stinkiest shoes.

179

A Canadian man can **DRILL** a **4.5-INCH** (11.4-cm) drill bit into his nose.

CATGUT = A TOUGH CORD MADE FROM ANIMAL INTESTINES USED TO STRING TENNIS RACKETS AND VIOLINS

AN ENGLISH ARTIST CREATED THE "BOGEY BALL" —A MOUND OF DRIED-UP BOOGERS HE SPENT TWO YEARS COLLECTING.

Seal **eyeballs** are **considered a special treat** for **Inuit children** in northern **Canada.**

A COMPANY IS BUILDING HOUSES IN INDONESIA USING BRICKS MADE OF COW DUNG.

OLD UNDERWEAR CAN BE RECYCLED AS STUFFING FOR COUCHES AND CAR SEATS.

A Burmese python once **exploded** after trying to digest an **alligator**.

In the 19th century, a **"rat-catcher"** earned money by collecting the rodents with his **bare hands.**

THE **LARGEST ORGANISM** ON **EARTH** IS THE

"HUMONGOUS FUNGUS."

SOME SEA SLUGS SHOOT TOXIC SNOT AT THEIR ENEMIES.

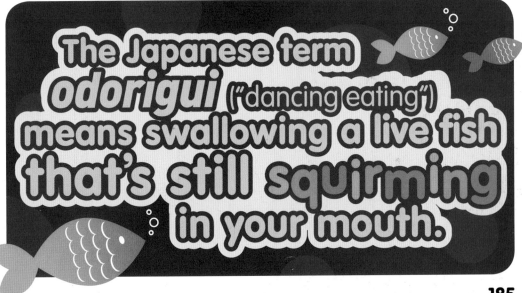

The Japanese term *odorigui* ("dancing eating") means swallowing a live fish that's still squirming in your mouth.

A COMPANY SELLS **SCORPION LOLLIPOPS** IN FLAVORS SUCH AS **BANANA, BLUEBERRY,** AND **APPLE.**

ASTRONAUTS HAVE LEFT NEARLY 100 BAGS OF **POOP, URINE, AND VOMIT** ON THE SURFACE OF THE **MOON.**

In some parts of China, people eat **monkey brains** with a side of pickled ginger and fried peanuts.

BURGERS MADE OF CRUSHED FLIES ARE POPULAR IN LAKE VICTORIA, AFRICA.

187

A performer nicknamed **Mr. Methane** can toot to the tune of the British national anthem.

A MAN HAD 13 POUNDS (6 KG) OF WARTS SURGICALLY REMOVED FROM HIS BODY.

In 1889, an inventor patented a locket you could use to stash your used chewing gum.

YOU CAN BRUSH YOUR TEETH WITH TOOTHPASTE FLAVORED LIKE

CURRY.

AT THANKSGIVING, ONE COMPANY SELLS A LIMITED-EDITION SODA FLAVORED LIKE **TURKEY** AND **GRAVY.**

Natto = a fermented soybean dish said to smell like sweaty socks

ONE CANDY COMPANY SELLS BACON-FLAVORED GUMBALLS.

An Italian fashion designer made dresses out of deli meats.

A STUDENT IN ENGLAND SOAKED IN A BATHTUB FULL OF COLD BAKED BEANS FOR TWO HOURS.

A MAN ONCE **BURIED HIMSELF** IN MORE THAN 10,000

EARTHWORMS
AND THEN **ATE SOME OF THEM** TO BREAK FREE.

A designer invented a lamp that runs on **human blood.**

Doctors once discovered a plant growing in a four-year-old boy's nose.

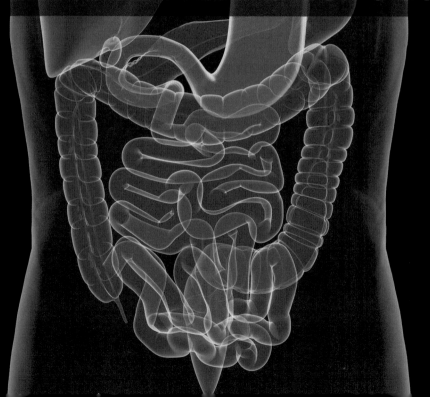

DOCTORS CAN CURE INTESTINAL INFECTIONS BY TRANSPLANTING A HEALTHY PERSON'S POOP INTO AN INFECTED PERSON'S GUT.

AN AMERICAN LONG-DISTANCE RUNNER HAD HIS TOENAILS PERMANENTLY REMOVED.

THOUSANDS of RATS

run amok inside the Karni Mata Temple in India.

(It's considered good luck if one scampers across your toes!)

Some Japanese ice-cream shops offer novelty flavors such as **slow-boiled egg** and **cow tongue.**

A CANADIAN ARTIST USES CHEWED GUM TO MAKE PORTRAITS OF CELEBRITIES.

25% OF BOTTLED WATER IS JUST TAP WATER.

FOR $425, YOU CAN BUY A PILL THAT WILL MAKE YOUR POOP SPARKLY GOLD.

FACT**FINDER**

Boldface indicates illustrations.

A

Airplane tray tables 51, **51**
Ambergris 116
"Angolan Jaw of Awe" **72–73,** 73
Antifreeze 155, **155**
Ants
    bites from 146, **146**
    colony size 21, **21**
    thief ants 95, **95**
    zombie ants 86, **86**
Argentine ants 21, **21**
Armor 152
Assassin bugs **32–33,** 33
Assassin spiders 46, **46**
Astronauts 92, 104–105, **104–105,**
    186, **186**

B

Baby poop 84
Bacon-flavored gumballs 190, **190**
Bacteria
    airplane trays 51, **51**
    belly button 26, **26**
    cheese and shoes 147
    floors 146
    mouth 31
    sofas 20
    and sweat 35
    toilets 99, **99**
    toothbrushes 80, **80**
Baked beans 191, **191**
Baked goods 55
Baldness 89
Baseball 64–65, **64–65**
Bathing
    avoiding 68
    in baked beans 191, **191**

    in blood 88
    as unhealthy 151
    in waste water 89
Bathroom behavior 95, 145
Bats 93, **93**
Beaches 56, **56,** 162, **162**
Beauty treatments 138, **139,** 151,
    151, 165
Beavers 54, **54**
Bedbugs 22, 114, **114**
Beds 67, **67**
Bees 144, **144**
Belly buttons 26, **26,** 79, **79**
Berry flavoring 54
Bird's nest soup 13, **13**
Black pudding 98, **98**
Bladder 75, **75**
Blindness 135
Blood
    bathing in 88
    in bedbug poop 114
    birds drinking 69
    Churchill's 136
    drinking 108
    in eyes of dwarf boas 113
    horned toads 21
    lamps powered by 192, **192**
    and leeches 172
    sausage made from 98, **98**
    in space 92
    squirting 15
    vampire bats 93, **93**
Blood sweat 101
Bloodletting 172–173
Blue whales 109
Bog snorkeling 163, **163**
"Bogey ball" (boogers) 181, **181**
Bombardier beetles 27
Boogers
    booger shooting contest 166

    collection 181, **181**
    contents 151
    elephant 168
Botfly larvae 27
Brains **94, 171**
    eating 171, 186
    in medicines 160
    parasitic worms in 94
    removal 89
    texture 37
    as toothpaste 76
Bread 158, **158**
Brooch, made of teeth 44
Bubble gum **100**
    auctioned off 64, **64**
    bacon-flavored 190, **190**
    celebrity portraits in 198
    jewelry 188
    removal 100
    wall of 157, **157**
Bug Bowl (competition) 175
Burgers 51, **51,** 63, 187, **187**
Burmese pythons 182, **182**
Burps 31, 44, 82, 115
Burrowing owls **18–19,** 19
Buses 5, **5**

C

Camels 82, **82**
Canada geese 10–11, **10–11**
Cars 70, **70**
Catgut 180
Celebrity portraits, from gum 198
Chamber pots 113, **113**
Chewing gum **100**
    auctioned off 64, **64**
    bacon-flavored 190, **190**
    celebrity portraits in 198
    jewelry 188

removal 100
wall of 157, **157**
Chiggers 132
China, ancient 174
Churchill, Winston 136
Clothes 74, 108, 190, **190**
Cockroaches 37, **37**, 68, **68**, 143, **143**
Cooking oil 83
Corpse flowers 21, **21**
Couches (sofas) 20, **20**, 182, **182**
"Cow chip" throwing competition 67
Cows **158**
    brains as food 171, **171**
    methane gas from 115
    poop 67, **67**, 158, 181, **181**
Cricket-spitting contest 175, **175**
Crocodiles 17, 84–85, **84–85**, 97
Curry-flavored toothpaste 189, **189**

D

Dead bodies
    and bugs 47, **47**
    curing cysts and warts 75, **75**
    exploding 84, **84**
    preserved 176
    stealing teeth from 81
Dentures 81
Divers and diving 66, **66**
Dress, made of meat 190, **190**
Drilling, into nose 180
Dung beetles **18–19**, 19, 28, **28–29**
Durians 96, **96**
Dust 110–111, 178
Dwarf boas 113
Dyes and dyeing 74, 76

E

Ears
    bedbug in 22

ear hairs 61, **61**
    implantation in arm 177, **177**
    infested with maggots 166
Earthworms 36, **36**, 174, **174**, 192
Earwax
    blue whales 109
    as lip balm 141
    mites eating rabbits' 35
    used for diagnosis 161, **161**
Egypt, ancient 66, 88–89, 151, **151**
Elephants 168, **168**
"Eskimo ice cream" 53, **53**
Estonian bagpipes 75, **75**
Exploding barn 115
Exploding bodies 84, **84**, 87, **87**, 182
Eye makeup 151, **151**
Eyelashes 58, **58**
Eyelids pulling cars 70, **70**
Eyes
    blood filled (Dwarf boas) 113
    blood-shooting (toads) 21, **21**
    crocodile foam 85
    eating 181
    found on beach 162, **162**
    popping from socket 79
    pupil enlargement 106, **106**

F

Falling worms 165, **165**
Feet 79, 179
Fingernails 71, **71**, 178, **178**
Fire ants 146, **146**
Fish
    eaten alive 185, **185**
    louse-infested 125
    scales in makeup 165
    sucked in and snorted out 63, **63**
Fist bumps 34
Five-second rule 146

Flavorings and additives
    from antifreeze 155, **155**
    from beavers' behinds 54
    from bugs' bellies 51
    from human hair 55
Flies 4, **4**, 164, 166
Fly burgers 187, **187**
Food
    beaver excretions as flavoring 54
    bird's nest soup 13, **13**
    black pudding 98, **98**
    brains as 171, **171**
    burgers 51, **51**, 63, 187, **187**
    dried frog guts 14
    durian 96, **96**
    earthworm soup 174, **174**
    "Eskimo ice cream" 53, **53**
    flavorings and additives 51, 54,
        55, 155, **155**
    fly burgers 187, **187**
    forty-year-old Twinkie 61, **61**
    haggis 81, **81**
    hot dogs 94, **94**
    human hair in 55
    ice cream 53, **53**, 198, **198**
    insects as 62, **62**, 63, 68, 161, **161**
    Jell-O 58, **58**
    live cockroaches as 68
    live fish as 185
    maggots as 109, **109**
    Modern Toilet Restaurant 57, **57**
    monkey brains as 186
    mushrooms 9, **9**
    natto 190, **190**
    peacocks as 154, **154**
    peanut butter 163, **163**
    pigs' feet 66
    prepared with feet 179
    regurgitated **128**, 128–129

scorpion lollipops 186, **186**
seal eyeballs as 181
snake's beating heart as 52, **52**
sweetbreads 167, **167**
tea, from poop 9
turkey-flavored soda 189, **189**
wormzels 69, **69**
Football 9, 61, **61**
Forensic entomologists 47
Fossilized vomit 147
Freckles 97, **97**
Frogs
    eaten by Venus flytrap 45, **45**
    eating shed skin 140, **140**
    as food 14
    swallowing method 125
Fungus 86, 184, **184**

G

Gas (toots)
    cow 115
    manatees 17
    musical 188, **188**
    per day 23
    termites 87
Generator, pee-powered 12, **12**
Germs 8, 34, 145
Giant African land snails 113, **113**
Giant water bugs 161
Giraffes 118, **118**
Gonzalez, Luis 64
Grasshoppers 63, **63**, 161, **161**
Greece, ancient 161
Guinea worms 136, **136**
Gum
    auction price 64, **64**
    bacon-flavored 190, **190**
    celebrity portraits from 198
    jewelry for storage 188

removal from sidewalks 100, **100**
wall of 157, **157**

H

Hagfish 17, **17**
Haggis 81, **81**
Hair
    in baked goods 55, **55**
    baldness prevention 89
    dyes 76
    ear hair 61, **61**
    growth locations 145, **145**
    jewelry made from 178
    museum displays 120, **120**
    rodent hairs in peanut butter 163
Hair balls 38, 66, **66**, 166
Hákarl (fermented shark meat) 59
Hamburgers 51, **51**, 63, 187, **187**
Hand-washing 145
Handshakes 34
Head lice 14, **14**
Headaches 156, **156**
Heart 15
Hippocrates 161
Hippos 101, **101**
Hook-worms 143, **143**
Horned owls 160, **160**
Horned toads 21, **21**
Horns 151, **151**
Horse racing 69, **69**
Hot dogs 94, **94**
Hotel rooms 8
Human body
    belly button 26, **26**
    bladder 75, **75**
    blood 15
    boogers 151
    brain 37
    hair 145, **145**

heart 15
mouth 31
mucus 16, 151
preserved 176
skin shedding 4
small intestine 27, **27**, 134, **134**
spit 126
stomach acid 142
tooting 23
"Humongous fungus" 184, **184**

I

Ice cream 53, **53**, 198, **198**
Iguanas 24, **24–25**
International Nose Picking Day 98
Intestines
    diseases 144, 194, **194**
    hook worms 143, **143**
    size 27, **27**, 134, **134**
    uses for 180

J

Jell-O 58, **58**
Jewelry 44, 178, 188

K

Karni Mata Temple, India 197
Ketchup 67, **67**
Kissing bugs 20, **20**
Knights 152
Koalas 124, **124**

L

Lamps 192, **192**
Leeches 172–173, **172–173**
Leopard geckos 127, **127**
Lice 125
Limburger cheese 147

Lions 38, **38–39**
Lip balm 141
Lollipops 63, 186, **186**
London, England 83, **83**
Louis XIV, King (France) 149
Louse 125
Lucas, James 68

M

Maggots
    in ears 166
    eating 109, **109**
    in mushrooms 9, **9**
    under skin 27
    treating wounds with 174
Makeup 151, **151,** 165
Manatees 16
Marine iguanas 24, **24–25**
Mattresses 67, **67**
Meat dresses 190, **190**
Methane gas 115
Mice 83, **83,** 158, **158, 163**
Mites
    dust 67, 110–111, **110–111**
    eating ear ooze 35
    in eyelashes 58
    in mushrooms 9, **9**
Modern Toilet Restaurant,
        Kaohsiung, Taiwan 57
Monkeys 112, **112,** 186
Moon 186, **186**
Morbid Anatomy Museum, Brooklyn,
        New York, U.S.A. 44
Mosquitoes 133, **133**
Motorized toilet 96, **96**
Mouth
    "Angolan Jaw of Awe" **72–73,** 73
    animal tongues 118, **118,** 125
    bacteria 31, **31**
    bugs bitting 20, **20**
    turtles peeing from 141
    see also Teeth
Mr. Methane 188, **188**
Mucus 16, 151, 176
Mummies 89, 100
Mushrooms 9, **9**
Mütter Museum, Philadelphia,
        Pennsylvania, U.S.A. 22

N

Nails
    fingernails 71, **71**
    jewelry from clippings 178, **178**
    toenails 44, **44,** 123, 195, **195**
Natto 190, **190**
Needles 78, **78**
New World screwworm 41, **41**
New York City, New York, U.S.A. 42–43,
        42–43
Nigeria, inventions by girls 12
Nile River, Africa 89
Nose
    boogers 151, 166, 168, 181, **181**
    drilling into 180
    leech living in 172
    mucus 16
    picking 98, 122, **122,** 159
    plant growing in 193, **193**
    toxic snot 185

O

Odorigui (swallowing live fish) 185
Opossums 35, **35**
Owls
    burrowing **18–19,** 19
    horned 160, **160**
    pellets 108

P

Paleoscatologists 60
Pandas 9, **9**
Pap (koala food) 124
Paper 153
Parasitic worms
    in brains 94
    Guinea worm 136, **136**
    hook-worms 143, **143**
    ingesting eggs of 144
Paris, France 107, **107**
Peacocks 154, **154**
Peanut butter 163, **163**
Pee (urine)
    annual quantity 117
    in armor 152
    bladder capacity 75, **75**
    chamber pots 113
    for fabric dyeing 74
    generator powered by 12, **12**
    on hands 65
    leopard geckos 127
    sharks 102
    in swimming pools 48–49
    as tooth whitener 76, **76**
    turtles 141
    vultures 80
Penguins **128,** 129
Perfumes 116, **116**
Peru, ancient 156
"Pestaurants" 63
Phones 95, **95,** 155
"Pie-scraper" (burger) 51, **51**
Pigs' feet, eating 66
Pimples 68
Pizza sauce 164
Plant, growing in nose 193, **193**
Plastinarium, Guben, Germany 176
"Poonado" 66

FACT**FINDER**

Poop
　baby's first 84
　as bait 18–19
　during battle 152
　beaches made from 56, **56**
　bedbugs 114
　bus powered by 5
　Canada geese 10–11
　cows 67, **67,** 158, 181, **181**
　desserts shaped like 57, **57**
　drinking water made from 94
　and dung beetles 28, **28–29**
　fossilized 60
　houses made from 181, **181**
　koalas 124
　pandas 9
　paper made from 153
　rhinos 6–7
　sculptures 148, **148–149**
　skipper caterpillars 136
　sloths 131
　snails in 50
　sparkly 199
　tea made from 9
　termite nests of 31
　treating infections with 194, **194**
　used for diagnosis 161
　whales 66
　wombats 121, **121**
Preserved bodies 176

R

Rats
　in Karni Mata Temple, India
　　196–197, 197
　in New York City **42–43,** 43
　rat-catchers 183, **183**
　in sewers 42
　squeezing in holes 83

　vomiting 42–43
Restaurants
　Modern Toilet Restaurant 57, **57**
　"pestaurants" 63
　"pie-scraper" burger 51, **51**
　urinal booths 107, **107**
Rhinos 6–7, **6–7,** 90, **90–91**
Ribbon worms 85, **85**
Roadkill 30, 169
Rome, ancient 76–77, 160
Rotorua, New Zealand 176
Rotten Sneaker Contest 179, **179**

S

Salad dressing 155
Salt, sneezing 24
Sandwiches 179, **179**
Scabs 123
Scorpions 170, **170,** 186, **186**
Screwworms 41, **41**
Scuba divers 66, **66**
Sculpture, dog poop 148, **148–149**
Sea cucumbers 115, **115,** 150, **150**
Sea pigs 150, **150**
Sea slugs 185
Seals 75
Sewers 42, 83, 107, **107**
Sharks 59, **59,** 102, **102–103**
Sheep 81, **81,** 153, **153**
Shrunken heads 40, **40**
Skin
　in dust 178
　frogs shedding 140
　humans shedding 4
　pickled 22
　sharks peeing through 102
Skipper caterpillars 136, **136**
Sloths 130–131, **130–131**
Slugs 119

Small intestine 27, **27,** 134, **134**
Smells
　corpse flower 21, **21**
　durian 96, **96**
　invented 14, **14**
　natto 190, **190**
　Rotorua, New Zealand 176
　rotting flesh 143
　shoes 179, **179**
　sweat 35
Snails
　in bird poop 50, **50**
　as cough syrup 156
　eating houses 113, **113**
　in spa treatments 138, **139**
Snakes 52, **52,** 113
Sneakers 147, **147**
Sneezes 24, 120, 132
Snorkeling 163, **163**
Snot, toxic 185
Soda 189, **189**
Sofas (couches) 20, **20,** 182, **182**
Soldiers 108, 152
Space 92
Spanish ribbed newts 117, **117**
Sparkly poop 199
Sperm whales 116
Spiders 46, **46,** 133
Spit 13, 82, 126
Spitballs 64, **64**
Stomach
　bagpipes made from 75
　haggis made from 81, **81**
　mucus in 176, **176**
　stomach acid 142
Stonie, Matt 94
Sugar 135, **135**
Sweat 35, 61, **61**
Sweetbreads 167, **167**

Swimming pools 48–49, **48–49**

T

Tea, from poop 9
Tears 144, **144**
Teenagers 122, **122,** 166
Teeth
    dentures from stolen teeth 81
    jewelry 44, 178, **178**
    toothbrushes 80, **80**
    toothpastes 76, 104, 189, **189**
    whitener 76, **76**
Termites 31, **31,** 87
Thief ants 95, **95**
Throne, toilet shaped like 149, **149**
Tickbirds 90, **90–91**
Toe jam 137, **137**
Toenails **44**
    chewing 123
    jewelry made from 178, **178**
    permanent removal of 194, **194**
    world's largest collection 44
Toilets
    chamber pots 113, **113**
    flushing 99, **99**
    and hand-washing 145
    of Louis XIV 149, **149**
    motorized 96, **96**
    open-air 77
    phone dropped in 155
    seat 20
    toilet paper 77
    on trains 119
Tongues (animal) 118, **118,** 125
Tooth whitener 76, **76**
Toothbrushes 80, **80**
Toothpaste 76, 104, 189, **189**
Toots
    cow 115

manatees 17
musical 188, **188**
per day 23
termites 87
Torupills (bagpipes) 75, **75**
Toxic snot 185, **185**
Trains 119, **119**
Tufted titmouse 30, **30**
Turkey-flavored soda 189, **189**
Turkey vultures 143
Turtles 141, **141**
Tut, King (Egypt) 89
Twinkies 61, **61**

U

Underwear 89, **89,** 182, **182**
Urinals 107, **107**
Urine (pee)
    annual quantity 117
    in armor 152
    bladder capacity 75, **75**
    chamber pots 113
    for fabric dyeing 74
    generator powered by 12, **12**
    on hands 65
    leopard geckos 127
    sharks 102
    in swimming pools 48–49
    as tooth whitener 76, **76**
    turtles 141
    vultures 80

V

Vampire bats 93, **93**
Vampire finches 69
Vampire spiders 133
Venus flytraps 45, **45**

Vomit
    crocodiles 97
    in football 9
    fossilized 147
    houseflies 4
    owl pellets 108, **108**
    penguins **128,** 129
    rats 42–43
"Vomit comet" (flight simulator) 105
Vultures 80, **80,** 143

W

Warts 75, 188, **188**
Water 89, 94, **94,** 198
Water bugs 161
Whales 66, **66,** 109, 116
William the Conqueror, King (England)
        84
Winter 108
Wombats 121, **121**
World Pigs' Feet Eating
        Championship 66
Worms
    earthworm soup 174, **174**
    falling from sky 165, **165**
    man buried in 192, **192**
    parasitic 94, 136, **136,** 143, **143,**
        144
    pretzels made of 69, **69**
    regrowing body parts into new
        worms 85, **85**
    tunneling into flesh 41
Wormzels 69, **69**

Z

Zombie ants 86, **86**

The publisher would like to thank all who worked to make this book come together: Julie Beer and Sarah Wassner Flynn, writers; Jennifer Agresta, project manager; Becky Baines, project editor; Lisa Jewell, photo editor; Michaela Weglinski, special projects assistant, editorial; Rachel Kenny, design production assistant; Callie Bonaccorsy, special projects assistant, design; Grace Hill, managing editor; Alix Inchausti, production editor.

Since 1888, the National Geographic Society has funded more than 12,000 research, exploration, and preservation projects around the world. The Society receives funds from National Geographic Partners, LLC, funded in part by your purchase. A portion of the proceeds from this book supports this vital work.

For more information, visit www.nationalgeographic.com, call 1-800-647-5463, or write to the following address:
National Geographic Partners, LLC
1145 17th Street N.W.
Washington, D.C. 20036-4688 U.S.A.

Visit us online at nationalgeographic.com/books

For librarians and teachers: ngchildrensbooks.org

More for kids from National Geographic: kids.nationalgeographic.com

For information about special discounts for bulk purchases, please contact National Geographic Books Special Sales: ngspecsales@ngs.org

For rights or permissions inquiries, please contact National Geographic Books Subsidiary Rights: ngbookrights@ngs.org

Paperback ISBN: 978-1-4263-2335-5
Reinforced library binding ISBN: 978-1-4263-2336-2

Printed in the United States of America
15/QGT-RRDML/1

PHOTO CREDITS

Cover: (blob fish), Kerryn Parkinson/ZUMAPRESS/Newscom; (cockroaches), Revensis/Dreamstime; (gum on shoe), Africa Studio/Shutterstock; (BACK), Ramona Kaulitzki/Shutterstock; spine, Revensis/Dreamstime

Illustrations throughout by Julide Obuz Dengel, Callie Bonaccorsy, and Maduza Design; 1 (cockroaches), Nengloveyou/Dreamstime.com; 1 (right), Africa Studio/Shutterstock; 2 (LO), Kerryn Parkinson/ZUMAPRESS/Newscom; 2-3 (cockroaches), Nengloveyou/Dreamstime.com; 4, r.classen/Shutterstock; 6-7, Djerasmus/Dreamstime.com; 9 (LO RT), Eric Isselée/Shutterstock; 10-11, Elliotte Rusty Harold/Shutterstock; 13, Fletcher & Baylis/Science Source; 17, Norbert Wu/Science Faction/Corbis; 18-19, Tom Vezo/Nature Picture Library; 19 (LO RT), Photobee/Dreamstime.com; 20 (LO), The Natural History Museum/Alamy; 21 (LE), Avmedved/Dreamstime.com; 21 (UP RT), Robin Treadwell/Science Source; 21 (LO), John Cancalosi/ARDEA; 24-25, Mark Carwardine/Nature Picture Library; 28-29, Cooper5022/Dreamstime.com; 30, William Leaman/Alamy; 31, Sydeen/Dreamstime.com; 32, Ra'id Khalil/Shutterstock; 35, Joe McDonald/Corbis; 36, Fishbgone/Dreamstime.com; 37, Nengloveyou/Dreamstime.com; 38-39, Debbie Christophers/National Geographic Creative/Corbis; 42-43, Songquan Deng/Shutterstock; 45, Chris Mattison/FLPA/Minden Pictures; 48-49, Chad Ehlers/Alamy; 51, Cavendish Press/Splash News/Newscom; 52 (LE), Czalewski/Dreamstime.com; 52 (BACK), homydesign/Shutterstock; 53 (UP), AP Photo/Al Grillo; 53 (LO), M. Unal Ozmen/Shutterstock; 54, National Geographic Creative/Getty Images; 56 (BACK), Socrates/Dreamstime.com; 56 (LO LE), NatalieJean/Shutterstock; 56 (UP), Cigdem Sean Cooper/Shutterstock; 57, Reuters/Nicky Loh; 58, Quayside/Dreamstime.com; 62, StockFood/Westend61; 64-65, Walleyelj/Dreamstime.com; 64 (UP), AdShooter/Getty Images; 67, yogesh more/Alamy; 68, smuay/Shutterstock; 69, Agencja Fotograficzna Caro/Alamy; 70, Dongzi - CNImaging/Newscom; 71, AP Photo/Seth Wenig; 72, WENN.com/Newscom; 78, Xin A i - CNImaging/Newscom;80, Musat/Dreamstime.com; 81, Paulcowan/Dreamstime.com; 83 (UP LE), CreativeNature R. Zwerver/Shutterstock;83 (CTR RT), Yeko Photo Studio/ Shutterstock; 83 (LO RT), Picsfive/Shutterstock; 86, Patrick Landmann/Science Source; 89 (LO), jocic/Shutterstock; 90-91, Bill Raften/Getty Images; 93, Kentoh/Dreamstime.com; 95, Ajay Kumar/Alamy; 96 (UP), Arisanjaya/Dreamstime.com; 96 (LO), AFP/Getty Images; 98, Pat-swan/Dreamstime.com; 101, NHPA/Photoshot/Newscom; 102-103, National Geographic Creative/Getty Images; 104-105, NASA; 106, Anemone/Shutterstock; 107, WENN.com/Newscom; 108 (UP), Ionia/Shutterstock; 108 (LO RT), Philippe Clement/Nature Picture Library; 110-111, Sebastian Kaulitzki/Shutterstock; 112, Aconcheng/Dreamstime.com; 113, Isselée/Dreamstime.com; 115, Mint Images RM/Getty Images; 117, age fotostock/Alamy; 118, megscapturedtreasures/Shutterstock; 121, Marco Tomasini/Dreamstime.com; 122, Artistan/Dreamstime.com; 124, Eric Isselée/Shutterstock; 127, Reinhold Leitner/Shutterstock; 128, Enrique R Aguirre Aves/Getty Images; 130-131, Vilainecrevette/Shutterstock; 133, Roger Eritja/Getty Images; 135, roblan/Dreamstime.com; 136, Rick & Nora Bowers/Alamy; 139, Franck Robichon/EPA/Newscom; 141, Think4photop/Dreamstime.com; 143 (LE), Science Picture Co./Corbis; 143 (LO RT), Science Photo Library/Getty Images; 145, 3445128471/Shutterstock; 146, Nature Picture Library/Alamy; 148-149, AP Photo/Vincent Yu; 149, Gauri Kulkarni Suryawanshi; 150, David Wrobel/Visuals Unlimited/Corbis; 154, Matej Kastelic/Shutterstock; 156, Photo Researchers RM/Getty Images; 157, Village Production/Getty Images; 158, Eric Isselée/Shutterstock; 160, Stephen Mcsweeny/Dreamstime.com; 161 (UP CTR), wonderisland/Shutterstock; 161 (UP RT), Rick Rhay/Getty Images; 161 (LO LE), ilolab/Shutterstock; 161 (LO CTR), kzww/Shutterstock; 163 (LE), United National Photographer/REX/Newscom; 163 (UP RT), Verastuchelova/Dreamstime.com; 164 (BACK), Andrey_Kuzmin/Shutterstock; 166, r.classen/Shutterstock; 168, Talvi/Shutterstock; 170, MRS.Siwaporn/Shutterstock; 172-173, Galamik/Dreamstime.com; 179, Ajn/Dreamstime.com; 182 (LE), Bildagentur-online/McPhoto/Alamy; 182 (RT), Chris Mattison/Alamy; 184, Els Branderhorst/Buiten-beeld/Minden Pictures/Corbis; 186, Sean Gallup/Getty Images; 188, Photo by J. Quinton/WireImage/Getty Images; 190 (UP LE), Aflo Co., Ltd./Alamy; 190 (LO RT), AP Photo/Mark Duncan; 191, jeehyun/Shutterstock; 194, iStock.com; 196-197, Wildcat78/Dreamstime.com

If you're not TOTALLY grossed out by now, you will be!

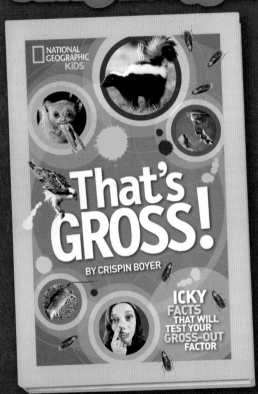

From dung-eating bugs to bug-eating humans, get ready to cringe, gag, and squirm while reading the most disgustingly awesome, totally true stories in *That's Gross!*

Discover **MORE** fun where **THAT** came from in the amazing That's series.